The Gift

I

Published by Adventurous Publishing

Hardback ISBN: 978-1-913310-35-6
Paperback ISBN: 978-1-913310-59-2

My intention behind writing this book is to inspire positive change and whatever that may look like.

In the form of a story, based on the life of a boy, a teacher and life's greatest lessons. I hope this book inspires you to be the best that you can be; I wish you endurance in times of failure and humility in times of triumph, and the very best in all your endevours.

DEDICATION

I'd like to dedicate this book to my family and friends; thank you for believing in me.

Introduction

In the quiet corners of our lives, lie the extraordinary moments that often go unnoticed, some encounters have the power to change the course of our existence. This is the story of one such encounter, a tale of a young boy named Benjamin Potter and the teacher who would shape his understanding of the world in profound ways.

Set against the backdrop of a small town in 1971, where the sun bathed the streets in golden warmth and life moved at a leisurely pace, young Benjamin's journey begins, As he embarks on the adventure of a new school, and stumbles upon the enigmatic Mr. Kolinsky, a physics teacher with a penchant for life's deepest mysteries.

As the pages of this story turn, you will accompany Benjamin on his quest for knowledge, wisdom, and purpose. You will witness the transformation of a timid boy into a young man of profound understanding, all under the guidance of a teacher who shares not only the secrets of the universe but also the secrets of the human heart.

Join us in this exploration of hope, forgiveness, and the enduring power of mentorship as we delve into the remarkable tale of Benjamin and Mr Kolinsky, a journey that will touch your soul and remind you of the profound impact one person can have on another's life.

Week One

The encounter

My name is Benjamin Potter. This book is about the quite abnormal gift I received from an unlikely sender when I was a boy. In turn, this is my gift to you; my story.

This story starts in 1971 when I was just thirteen years young; I remember waking up to the hollar of my rooster clock and the warm glaze of the sun. The smell of maple syrup and pancakes rushed up my nostrils; Mum had prepared my favourite, pancakes and syrup. I still remember how they tasted and the awful mess I made. She never complained, not once.

Arriving at the large timber doors of my new school, my teenage confidence departed, time slowed and my heart paced. Before my world caved in I took a quick detour to the bathroom before class. After dealing with finished cubical business and a short pep talk from the mirror, I rushed out of the bathroom and saw a muddy footstep on the floor. Looking further I saw a trail that led to a physics classroom. I thought I'd better check it out, stepping on a pair of brown leather shoes, I saw purple polka dot socks, black trousers, a blue chequered shirt, a distinct moustache, and a shiny, hairless head.

"Hello, young man. Are you all right?" He asked.
"Yes, thanks. Sorry about that, sir. I was following a mud trail."
"I guess gardening follows me everywhere." He chuckled.
"Well, I'm deeply sorry, I'm going to be late for my next class. Have a good day, sir."
"What lesson do you have first?" He asked, making a face with his eyebrows.
"Physics, in room A."
"You must be the new student they were telling me about. I'm Mr Kolinsky your new physics teacher."
"My name is Benjamin - Benjamin Potter. If I had friends, they'd call me Ben."
He quickly responded,
"Well, come on in, then, Ben. How about we start a bit early today?" he asked. "Sure!" I replied.
"What do you know about the world?" He asked curiously.
"I know the earth is round, and there are a couple billion..." - "No, no Ben, (he chuckled) not how many people there are or how round the earth is. What do you know about the world, natural laws, morals, ethics, people, and the real things that matter in life?"

WHAT DO YOU REALLY KNOW?

"Well, I know that there are good and bad people, humble and arrogant people," I answered.
"Good Ben, that's a great start. You mentioned good and bad people. How does someone become known as a 'bad' person?" He asked.
"Well from what I've been told, if they've committed a terrible crime or made a bad decision."
"That's great, Ben. You're getting the hang of this. I have one more question for you. What if I told you that most 'bad' people had key deficiencies in their upbringing?"
"But is a poor upbringing a good enough reason to commit murder or treacherous things, Mr Kolinsky?" I asked passionately. "Well, that's a good point Ben, one we should ponder about. What if people act the way they do because of how they were treated or the environment they grew up in? - for instance, in my garden. What if I neglected my flowers and ripped out their roots?"
"Well, that wouldn't be good," I replied.
"Of course, it wouldn't! - everything has a specific need, just like a flower. And if those needs aren't met, more often than not people tend to look for them elsewhere, particularly in not the best of places." He said with a grin.
"Are you saying people act the way they do because of what people have poured on them?"
"That's great, Ben, but more accurately, what's been poured into them. Ben, imagine each person on this earth starting out with empty cups, quite literally every interaction, each praise, or reprimand begins to fill that cup up, indefinitely growing up with the wrong ingredients being poured into this cup that person becomes bitter, selfish and begins to use their pain as a reason to blame and inflict suffering, rather than fuel to change. Albert Einstein once said nothing happens until something moves, quite When that something moves atoms collide creating a perpetual motion of never-ending movement, which means everything is related, converted and transported. A person's actions today are quite closely related to how they felt or were treated some time ago. The world is simpler than we think, and more understandable than we comprehend."

Before I understood what he meant, the school bell rang.

"Open your physics book to page one, please! Today we have a new student with us, and he's already become my friend after fifteen minutes. Meet Benjamin."
I stood up as my heart pounded against my ribs. "Hello, everyone. I squealed." The room stood quiet, so quiet I could hear my breath. They'll come along, Ben. Mr Kolinsky said quietly. I sat back in my seat. Soon after, I felt a soft thump on my shoulder. It was a note.

"Go back to where you came from."
I frantically looked around the classroom to see who had written it. I sunk into the frame of my chair. I couldn't wait until school finished. As soon as those bells rang, I ran straight out the school doors.

2

THE GIFT

The next day I woke up bright and early. Last night, I couldn't help but think about what Mr Kolinsky meant and what an empty cup had to do with someone being clever. I walked softly down the stairs, still thinking of what he meant. "Good Morning, mum. "Morning Ben; you seem suspiciously quiet this morning. "What's the catch, Pocket money? Well, What is it, Ben?" she asked while waving the spatula around. "Well, I've been thinking about what my teacher said to me. What does having an empty cup mean, mum?" "Well, it means dropping everything you think you know to learn something better, Ben. What subject does she teach?"
"Well, it's a He, and his name is Mr Kolinsky; he's a physics teacher, but what does that have to do with physics?" I asked curiously. "Well, you'll have to find out." She said with a mischievous grin. I threw on my jacket, wrestled with my shoes, and ran out the door. Ben! Benjamin! Your lunch. My mum shouted. Oh, thanks, mum. Have fun, Ben!

I ran up to the school stairs, opened the large doors, and ran straight to the physics classroom. Doom Boom, Doom. I knocked on the door and anxiously waited. The door slowly crept open. I saw Mr Kolinsky looking out the window at the beautiful sunrise. "Ben!" He exclaimed. "Good Morning Mr Kolinsky. I wondered if we could start class early again today, I've come with a question". "Oh, of course, Ben, I do love answering questions. Come on in." He said whilst sitting in his chair and taking a bite out of his apple.
How does one empty his cup? Oh, that's a great question, Ben! Well, emptying your cup is a part of the process, but the main thing that needs to happen before anything else is identifying what's already in the cup. Here's an example Ben I used to be in the army, and one of the main things we were taught was how to work as a unit; now, in a unit, there are several characters, you have the leader, the followers, the smart guys, the not-so-smart guys, and the people who posed as the problem. Now Ben, how did we identify who the problem was? Umm, because they didn't want to work as a unit? That's precisely right, Ben! - A problem in any situation that wants to avoid cooperating with the mission or goal at hand. So how do you get rid of that problem, Mr Kolinsky? Another great question Ben. A problem's greatest enemy is a solution followed by action. Most people spot a problem and identify it as a problem without doing anything. Isn't that similar to weeds growing in a garden? That's precisely right, Ben. Now, how do you deal with weeds, Ben? You cut them. I said unconfidently.

Well, that's close, Ben - how about going to the root? You see, a problem is always more significant than it might seem. For example, poverty just like maths poverty is an answer made up of a complex equation, the cause of poverty is a lack of determination.

Now, you must understand that determination and hard work are very different. A man may work hard for his whole life and still be poor, but a determined man will be rich and knowledgable, provided he can empty his cup. So are you saying people are poor because of a lack of determination? I asked. Well, Ben, a lack of determination is a minor factor in how people stay poor. Poverty essentially is a prison designed to keep people trapped inside.

For example, Ben, why do you think most betting shops and liquor stores are near poor people? - Ben, if you take a man's right to think, you've robbed him of his humanity, therefore leaving him trapped in the cycle. Well, how do people get out of that prison? I asked. Well, Ben. He sighed. Most people are in that "poverty prison" for life, while some hardly make it. Mr Kolinsky, if poverty is a prison, who's the authority? Governments, schools, and people, Ben, the very same people that employed me. Well, what does education have to do with poverty? Good question, Ben, well Why do you think there are such things as private schools, and what type of people go to them? People, who become leaders? That's precisely right Ben! -Now, what about the people that go to a state school? Followers. I replied. See, Ben, life is a game. You need to know how to play and how to play well.

Well, that's close, Ben - how about going to the root? You see, a problem is always more significant than it might seem. For example, poverty just like maths poverty is an answer made up of a complex equation, the cause of poverty is a lack of determination. Now, you must understand that determination and hard work are very different. A man may work hard for his whole life and still be poor, but a determined man will be rich and knowledgable, provided he can empty his cup. So are you saying people are poor because of a lack of determination? I asked. Well, Ben, a lack of determination is a minor factor in how people stay poor. Poverty essentially is a prison designed to keep people trapped inside.

For example, Ben, why do you think most betting shops and liquor stores are near poor people? - Ben, if you take a man's right to think, you've robbed him of his humanity, therefore leaving him trapped in the cycle. Well, how do people get out of that prison? I asked. Well, Ben. He sighed. Most people are in that "poverty prison" for life, while some hardly make it. Mr Kolinsky, if poverty is a prison, who's the authority? Governments, schools, and people, Ben, the very same people that employed me. Well, what does education have to do with poverty? Good question, Ben, well Why do you think there are such things as private schools, and what type of people go to them? People, who become leaders? That's precisely right Ben! -Now, what about the people that go to a state school? Followers. I replied. See, Ben, life is a game. You need to know how to play and how to play well.

Well, what about forgiveness Mr Kolinsky? What about it, Ben? Well, how does one start to forgive? Forgiveness is a big subject, more complicated than rocket science, but once experienced it can easily be understood. Come to me tomorrow a little earlier, Ben, and we'll have another chat.

On my way home from school, I kept thinking about what Mr Kolinsky had shared with me - I was starting to enjoy these conversations with him. I'd learned so much already; who knew that some physics teacher could teach you the physics of life? I couldn't wait for tomorrow and the conversation we would have.

THE GIFT

The following day, I woke bright and early, with yet another view of a beautiful sunrise through my bedroom window. "Good Morning, Mum!", I shouted. There was no response. Mum, hello. Hello Benjamin. It came from a deep voice. Hello, who are you? The man appeared in a military uniform - slowly taking off his cap, he said. It's me, your father, Benjamin. I finished my last tour. I'm here to stay now. He said. A tear rolled down the side of my cheek, red conquered my face, and my bones turned weak. Hello Dad, that is what I wanted to say, but the words wouldn't come out. I turned around, ran straight into my room, slammed the door, and sat down. Why didn't he even write? Not even a call? - Soon after my sadness had turned into anger, I kept repeating to myself, "I'll never forgive him."

I hadn't seen my dad since his first tour six years ago. I had almost forgotten what he looked like.

Boom, Doom, Boom. The door crept open. Hello Ben! Is this becoming a regular thing now? I immensely enjoy these conversations. Well, I do, too. So it is, then! - What are we talking about today? Oh yes, forgiveness. Yeah. Well, first of all, whom do you want to forgive? He asked curiously. My father, Donald Potter. Well, what has he done that's hurt you, Ben? We were fine until my sixth birthday when he got a call from them and left. Who's them, Ben? The Army. Oh, so I understand you're sad about your dad because of him leaving you? He didn't just leave me. He abandoned me. Did he not write to you? No. Not even a call? No, nothing. I thought he was dead. I understand. Surprisingly he came back from his tour today. Were you excited? Mainly angry, I wanted to hug him but was filled with rage. "Ben, let me tell you a story. There was once a great samurai master that lived in the mountains of Japan. One day a young warrior filled with hatred and revenge came to the master's home. The warrior bowed and embraced the master. The master was pleased. The warrior stood up and asked the master how to forgive and deal with his hatred because it devoured him daily."

The master stood up and started walking - the warrior followed.

"Young man, forgiveness is not about the other person. It's for you. If you fill yourself with hatred, it's like a poison that travels through the veins of your body. An instant kill is a luxury in the world of poison - this type of poison kills you painfully, slowly." The master explained.

"You see, Ben, forgiveness is a cure to the poison that will devour you in time if you don't."

"I enjoyed that story Mr. Kolinsky, but what if the person doesn't change?"

"The young warrior from the story asked the very same thing."

"Well, what did he say?" I asked inquisitively

"He said that person has a poison within them, just like you did, but you see if they continue not to change they will soon die, meaning depression, anger and hatred will take over. He said to the warrior, young man, trees also sustain the world's most wicked people. Life sustains life. So you should sustain other people.

Mr kolinsky went on to say..."What this means Ben is, you be the best person that you can be. Don't do to people what they do to you. Forgiving isn't an opportunity to move on it's an opportunity to build a better relationship."

Chapter Two

The Philomaths path

|fil-uh-math| *A lover of learning*, Noun.

Mr Kolinsky had always referred to life lessons as The Physics of Life. I always needed clarification on what he meant by that, but I would soon find out.

Doom, Boom, Doom. "Good Morning Mr Kolinsky," I said. " Hello, Ben! How are you today, young man?" He asked. "I'm good, thanks. What do you mean when you say, 'The Physics of Life?'

"Well, Benjamin, the physics of life is how I refer to how everything co-exists. Along with our purpose in this world. Which requires discipline." He said.

"What does discipline mean? I asked. "Discipline is teaching someone to follow certain rules or a code of behaviour. For example, in my military days, my company commander would always say, "If a man succeeds in executing a mission but fails to make his own bed, he has no discipline."

"What does discipline have to do with making your bed?"

"Good question Ben. I pondered the very same thing. Discipline starts at home. How you do one thing is how you do everything. Do you make your bed, Ben?

"Not always," I replied.

"Ben, starting tomorrow morning, I want you to make your bed."

"But how is that going to help me?" I asked. " Ben, the first step in becoming a good person overall is to be disciplined; discipline makes birds travel thousands of miles, and the world's greatest athletes run hundreds of meters; It's also what turns a boy into a man."

"What is a purpose, Mr Kolinsky? "
"A purpose, In short, is why me, you, and all other humans were put on this earth. He said.
"Well, are our purposes all the same?" I asked.
"That's a good question, Ben, but fortunately, they aren't. Each soul has a different purpose." He said. "Well, what's mine?" I asked, "Ben, I can't answer that question." he replied softly. "Who can?" Well, two people can answer that question." he said "Well, who?" I asked. "You and the creator." He answered.
"Before you go, Ben, remember that living the life of a philomath is most rewarding. It might even help you find your purpose."
After leaving school that day, I had to find out what a philomath was and how it might help me find my purpose. I figured that the library was the best place to start.

"Good Morning, young man. What can I help you with?" The librarian asked.

"I'm looking for a book on philomaths."

"Well, that's a new one, especially from someone your age. Aisle three, shelf number four." She said, scratching her head.

I walked to the aisle, reached up to shelf four and found a book called 'The Philomathical life' I sat down with my back against the aisle and started to read the first page read "In order to live a fulfilled life, one has to learn, grow and expand his knowledge, a man that knows not much, cannot change his ways." I think that quote means a person who doesn't know a lot is unable to change or grow due to their inability to become more knowledgeable.

I started to read and take notes of chapter one. ..

The word Philo means to love. To accept, and thereafter understand (e.g someone who loves learning). The conflict in the world of today, tomorrow and the indefinite past is the contrasting act of philosophical living. The missing factor in today's world is not the how the who or when but the if. If people really did think about the legacy that will shortly follow them, would they still do the bad they do now?

What if, the world's problem wasn't what we didn't know, but what we think we do?

What if, the world's biggest dilemmas could be solved, through the most microscopic changes?

Why does the word philo come before math?

Before I could finish the page there was an announcement.

"The library will be closing shortly, please make your way to the exit or to the librarian's desk if you wish to borrow a book."

I picked up my book and paced to the librarian's desk. Spinning his chair around whilst taking a puff out of his cigar he said

"Hey kid, what can I do for ya?"

The librarian was a skinny, young caucasian man. He had short light brown hair and couldn't have been older than twenty. He had the unmistakable voice of a radio personality.
Taking a seat I asked..
"Can I borrow this book?"
"Well sure, but since that's the only copy around you can only borrow it for up to a week at a time."
After strenuously clacking his keypad.
"It'll be a dollar, twenty." He said.
Digging my pockets I replied, " I don't have a dollar-twenty now, can I borrow the book and give it to you when I'm done?"

Lighting his cigar he said. "I'll tell you what, there's been a shortage of workers in the library, If you could help me out around here, that book is yours."

We shook hands and I headed home.

I biked home that day with a great sense of pride, it was as if a blip had been attached to the crown of my head. I couldn't wait to tell Mr Kolinsky what I had learnt.

Bang, bang, bang... " Hello, Ben!" He exclaimed. "Hello Mr Kolinsky, I found that book you were telling me about, the one on philomaths." "Well tell me, what have you learned?"
"I learned that the teachings of a philomath can be found in everyone, in musicians, athletes, and some of the world's smartest people. A *philomathical life* is formed upon love and thereafter understanding. The word *Philo* means to love, and *math* to study or learn. In order for a student to become a master in later days, love and acceptance for the teaching must come before comprehension and understanding it. The art of a philomath is found in the harmonies of music, the synchronised precise breaths of an athlete and the discipline of a great mathematician. A philomath is not an act, but a way of living, even, a way of life. "

CHAPTER 3

A LIFETIME OF PHYSICS

Over these past weeks, I've learnt a lot from Mr. Kolinsky, but I ceased to know anything about him, the thought of who he really was, where he grew up, and why he became a physics teacher started to *lurk*. In the grand scheme of it all, he was a big, bold question mark.

I popped by the physics department before my music class.

"Hello, Mr Kolinsky."

"Good morning Ben, What brings you by today?" he said almost lifeless.

"Mr. Kolinsky I've been trying to read the book that I got from the library but I couldn't help but wonder who you were, before physics, and how you seem to know everything. "

"So we've gotten there have we, have a seat." Tapping on a nearby chair.

"Tell me everything," -

Ploddingly, he started - "I was born on the *sixteenth* of *November nineteen-ten* to a well-earned family in south Idaho. My father Robert Kolinsky Sr. was a tall man with a distinctly bulky stature. He wore long brown hair and the beard of a true Renaissance man, his occupation was a world food import businessman and in his spare time a voracious reader. *Solid* man he was; an even better father. He would often tell me about how good of a batting arm he had on him when he was around your age."

Shuffling to the edge of my chair I asked, "What about your mother?"

"My mother Julia was a model, she came from a family of *artists* and *warheads*, so the opposites of worlds do meet eventually 'he chuckled'; *anyhoo* Julia Kolinsky Wetherhouse was her full name. Much like her name, there was *no one* like her. *Tearfully glancing at his mug* - She'd always leave her latest work on my bed each week after school, accompanied by a plate of pancakes and syrup; my favourite. I remember the smile on her face when she got her photo on the front page of a supercar magazine with her in the driver's seat of the world's fastest car at the time. As I think of it, my father didn't have all the looks but he sure did have standards. - *We both laughed.*

Growing up in an era of war and new order most parents shepherded their children to books on war and took up roles in the army or signed up at the local reserve, being the man that my father was, giving me a book on physics, was his way of showing the standard expected of my life to be. At times I despised the subject, but through my father's firm but understanding teaching and underlying respect for Oppenheimer I grew to love it. Day by day I grew stronger at physics and eventually surpassed all my teaching I was on my way to exceeding my father's expectations of me. While eating dinner one evening my parents told me the surprising news that I would be sent away to a physics boarding school to enhance my learning, At the time I thanked them but deep down, I was horrified.

My father had arranged for a car since the railway had been shut down due to frequent German bombings. The journey was long and tiring, but I was still grateful. Waking up to a light thump of my bag I peeked out the window, and before me was the most beautiful work of architecture I had seen. Long arrays of marble pillars supported the school's large structure, The ten acres of land it sat on were filled with smartly cut hedges and long pine trees, cut grass met a staircase to the large, engraved, wooden doors that awaited me.

Little did know that the black 1925 Cadillac sedan I arrived in would be the last car I would see for a long time."

"Inside the grand doors of the school, I was welcomed by the headmaster, Dr. William Lawrence. He was a tall, thin man with a sharp jawline and a stern expression. 'Welcome to the Lawrence Institute of Physics, Mr. Kolinsky, he said with a firm handshake.' 'Here, we nurture the brightest minds in the field of physics. You have a bright future ahead of you if you're willing to put in the effort." I was assigned to a room on the third floor of the dormitory. My roommate, James, was a fellow physics enthusiast, and we quickly became close friends. We spent countless nights discussing theories, experimenting with our own ideas, and pushing the boundaries of our understanding of the universe.

"Dr. Lawrence was a tough mentor. He pushed us to our limits, often giving us complex problems that seemed unsolvable. But he believed that the struggle to find solutions was where true learning occurred. He used to say, 'The process of solving a problem is just as important, if not more so, than the solution itself.'

"In my third year at the institute, World War II was in full swing. Many of my fellow students and professors left to serve in the war effort. I wanted to contribute too, but Dr. Lawrence insisted that my role was to continue my studies and eventually teach the next generation of physicists. He believed that knowledge was the most potent weapon of all. After the war ended, I returned to the institute to complete my studies. I had grown into a young man with a deep passion for physics and a burning desire to pass on my knowledge. Dr. Lawrence retired, and I took his place as the head of the physics department.

"Years went by, and I taught many students, each with their unique gifts and challenges. I learned that teaching was not just about imparting knowledge; it was about understanding the individual needs of each student, helping them empty their cups, and guiding them to find their purpose in the world.

"And that, Ben, is how I ended up here, as your physics teacher. My life has been dedicated to the pursuit of knowledge and the belief that every student has the potential to change the world if they are willing to learn, grow, and embrace the physics of life."

Chapter Four

The Weight

The following week crisp autumn had taken amist. Mr. Kolinsky entered the classroom with an air of excitement. He beckoned me to follow him, and we ventured beyond the confines of the classroom and the familiar hallways of the institute. It was a journey into the heart of nature itself.

We walked through the serene campus, the leaves crunching beneath our feet, their colours transforming the surroundings into a canvas of reds, yellows, and oranges. The air was filled with the earthy scent of fallen leaves, and the distant chirping of birds added a symphonic touch to the scenery. Mr. Kolinsky's moustache bristled with anticipation, and his eyes sparkled like a child about to unveil a hidden treasure.

We arrived at a small, secluded pond surrounded by ancient oak trees. A wooden bench sat beside it, offering a tranquil view of the water. A pair of swans gracefully glided across the pond's surface, leaving ripples in their wake. It was a scene of serene beauty, and I couldn't help but be captivated by it.

"Ben, do you see this pond?" Mr. Kolinsky asked, his voice soft and contemplative.

"Yes, it's beautiful," I replied, mesmerized by the scene.

"Indeed, it is," he said, his gaze fixed on the swans. "This pond, my boy, holds a lesson about hope."

Hope? I was intrigued. "What do you mean, Mr. Kolinsky?"

He gestured toward the swans. "You see those swans, Ben? They're a symbol of hope. Swans are known for their grace and beauty, but what's truly remarkable about them is their ability to remain calm and serene on the surface, even when they're paddling furiously beneath the water."

I never quite understood where all his knowledge came from but I strived to know everything Mr Kolinsky knew and more, The world would be merely a game if I had known everything.

I watched as the swans glided effortlessly across the pond, their movements so serene that it was easy to forget the powerful strokes hidden beneath the surface.

"Life, Ben, is much like those swans," Mr. Kolinsky continued. "We often face challenges, struggles, and obstacles that are hidden from view. But just like the swans, we have the power to remain calm on the surface, to exude grace and beauty, even when we're working hard to overcome our difficulties."

As I absorbed his words, I realized that Mr. Kolinsky was teaching me a lesson not just about physics but about life itself. Hope, he explained, was the ability to see beauty and grace in the midst of adversity, to believe in a better future even when the waters were rough.

"Remember, Ben," he said with a gentle smile, "in the darkest of times, it's hope that keeps us afloat. It's the belief that, no matter how tough the challenges, there's always a possibility of something beautiful waiting to emerge."

We sat in silence for a while, watching the swans as they continued their elegant dance on the pond. The lesson had left an indelible mark on me, a reminder that even in the most challenging moments of life, hope could be a beacon of light guiding us forward.

As we made our way back to the classroom, I couldn't help but feel a renewed sense of purpose and a deeper appreciation for the lessons Mr. Kolinsky imparted, not just in physics but in the profound physics of life. Each day with him was a journey of discovery, and I eagerly looked forward to the next lesson. The days turned into weeks, and my conversations with Mr. Kolinsky continued to shape my understanding of the world. We delved deeper into the philosophy of life, discussing topics like compassion, empathy, and the interconnectedness of all things. Mr. Kolinsky often used his garden as a metaphor for life's lessons. He would say, "Just as I tend to my garden, nurturing each plant and giving it what it needs to thrive, so too should we nurture our relationships and the world around us."

As we sat on the bench Mr. Kolinsky shared a story from his own life. He spoke of a time when he had faced a difficult decision during his military service. He had to choose between following orders that he believed were morally wrong or standing up for what he knew was right. It was a test of his principles and values, and he chose the latter, even though it came with great personal sacrifice.

"Ben," he said, "there will come moments in your life when you'll have to make choices that define who you are. It won't always be easy, and the path of righteousness may be filled with obstacles, but never compromise your principles. Be like a tree that stands tall, firmly rooted in its values."

As the school year progressed, I began to notice changes within myself. I had become more disciplined, taking charge of making my own bed every morning. I had also started volunteering at the library after school, helping the librarian organize books and assisting other students with their research. The librarian, whose name was Mr. Stevens, became a mentor of sorts, teaching me about the power of knowledge and the importance of sharing it with others.

One evening, while I was working at the library, a young boy approached me with a timid expression. He asked for help finding a book on a subject he was struggling with in school. I guided him to the right section and showed him a few relevant books. His eyes lit up with gratitude, and he said, "Thank you, sir. You're really nice."

Those words warmed my heart, and I couldn't help but smile. It was a small moment, but it made me realize the impact we can have on others when we extend a helping hand and share our knowledge. It was a lesson in empathy and compassion, a lesson Mr. Kolinsky had emphasized in our discussions.

As the school year came to a close, I found myself reflecting on the remarkable journey I had been on. I had not only learned about the laws of physics but had also discovered the profound wisdom of life. Mr. Kolinsky had been more than a teacher; he had been a guiding light, illuminating the path to understanding and enlightenment.

On the last day of school, I approached Mr. Kolinsky with a small gift—a potted plant for his garden. He accepted it with a smile and said, "Thank you, Ben. This plant will remind me of our time together and the growth we've both experienced."

With a sense of gratitude and hope, I bid farewell to my physics teacher and headed home. That summer, I continued my journey of learning, exploring new subjects, and sharing my knowledge with others. I knew that the gift Mr. Kolinsky had given me—the gift of understanding and hope—was something I would carry with me for the rest of my life.

As the days turned into weeks and weeks into months, Ben continued his journey of self-discovery and growth under the guidance of Mr. Kolinsky. Each day brought new lessons, conversations, and insights that expanded Ben's understanding of life's mysteries.

One sunny afternoon, as they sat on a bench in Mr. Kolinsky's garden, the old teacher shared another story from his own life. This time, he spoke of a journey he had undertaken in his youth, a journey that had shaped him into the man he had become.

"It was a journey of exploration and self-discovery," Mr. Kolinsky began. "I was just a young man back then, full of dreams and curiosity. I decided to embark on a solo expedition into the heart of the Amazon rainforest. It was a place of unparalleled beauty and danger, a place where one could lose themselves in the vastness of nature."

Ben listened intently, captivated by the images Mr. Kolinsky's words painted in his mind. He could almost hear the sounds of the rainforest, the chirping of birds, and the rustling of leaves.

"I spent months in the jungle, learning from indigenous tribes, studying the flora and fauna, and facing the challenges of survival," Mr. Kolinsky continued. "But it was during a particularly difficult moment that I learned one of life's most valuable lessons."

He paused as if reliving the memory. Ben leaned closer, eager to hear more.

"I had ventured deep into the rainforest, far away from any civilization. I encountered a massive waterfall, a sight of breathtaking beauty. But I was determined to climb it, to conquer it. I thought it would be a symbol of my strength and courage."

Ben's eyes widened in anticipation.

"I began the ascent, and for a while, everything went smoothly. But as I climbed higher, the terrain became treacherous. The rocks were slippery, the water rushed with incredible force, and the height was dizzying. I was determined not to give up, but the waterfall seemed unconquerable."

Mr. Kolinsky's voice softened. "That's when I realized the futility of my ego-driven quest. I was risking my life for a meaningless accomplishment, something that no one would ever witness or care about. It was then that I made a choice."

Ben held his breath, waiting for the revelation.

"I chose to turn back. I chose life over ego, wisdom over recklessness. I descended the waterfall and returned to safer ground. It was a humbling experience, a reminder that not every challenge is meant to be conquered, and not every risk is worth taking."

The two sat in silence for a moment, absorbing the profound lesson. Ben couldn't help but think of his own journey and the challenges he had faced. He realized that, like Mr. Kolinsky, he had choices to make about how he would navigate life's complexities.

Chapter Four
-A heartfelt connection

As my journey of self-discovery continued, I found myself drawn to the question of purpose. It was a question that had been on my mind ever since Mr. Kolinsky had mentioned it.

One day, as we strolled through the garden, I turned to my teacher. "Mr. Kolinsky, you once said that our purpose in life is something only we and the creator can determine. But how do we discover it? How do we know what our purpose is?"

Mr. Kolinsky smiled, his eyes twinkling with wisdom. "Discovering one's purpose is a lifelong journey, Ben. It's not something that can be rushed or forced. It often reveals itself through a series of experiences, challenges, and moments of clarity."

I frowned, feeling a bit lost. "So, how do I even begin to uncover my purpose?"

Mr. Kolinsky placed a reassuring hand on my shoulder. "Start by following your passions and interests. Explore what brings you joy and fulfilment. Pay attention to the moments when you feel most alive and aligned with your true self."

I nodded, a sense of hope blossoming within me. "And what if I don't find my purpose right away?"

In the following weeks, I delved deeper into my studies, immersing myself in books, research, and the pursuit of knowledge. I had become a true philomath, a lover of learning, just as Mr. Kolinsky had encouraged me to be.

One day, while browsing through a library, I stumbled upon a quote that resonated deeply with me: "In order to live a fulfilled life, one has to learn, grow, and expand their knowledge. A person who knows not much cannot change their ways."

I shared the quote with Mr. Kolinsky, who smiled approvingly. "That quote, Ben, encapsulates the essence of a philomath's path. It's about the relentless pursuit of knowledge, not just for the sake of knowledge but for personal growth and transformation."

Inspired by the quote, I continued my studies with renewed vigour. I began to see the world through the lens of a lifelong learner, finding wonder and curiosity in every corner of life.

With each passing day, I found myself immersed in a world of knowledge and contemplation. Mr. Kolinsky continued to be my guiding light, offering insights and wisdom that shaped my understanding of life.

One afternoon, as we sat in his study surrounded by books that seemed to hold centuries of wisdom, I asked, "Mr. Kolinsky, how do you accumulate such a wealth of knowledge? It's awe-inspiring."

He chuckled softly. "The pursuit of knowledge, my dear friend, is a lifelong endeavour. Every book, every conversation, every moment of reflection adds a piece to the puzzle. But remember, wisdom is not just about the accumulation of facts. It's about understanding, empathy, and the ability to see the interconnectedness of all things."

His words resonated deeply within me. I realized that true wisdom was not confined to the pages of books but was a living, breathing force that flowed through the experiences and teachings of those who came before us.

As the weather changed once more so did the scenery, I found myself reflecting on the threads that wove the tapestry of my life. There were moments of joy and laughter, moments of sorrow and introspection, and moments of profound connection with Mr. Kolinsky.

One evening, as we sat by the fireplace, I said, "Mr. Kolinsky, I've come to realize that life is like a tapestry, intricate and beautiful, woven together by the threads of our experiences. Each thread, whether bright or dark, adds to the richness of the whole."

He nodded in agreement. "Indeed, life's tapestry is a masterpiece, and we are both the weavers and the threads. Embrace every color, every texture, for they all contribute to the unique pattern that is yours alone."
I gazed into the dancing flames, contemplating the profound truth of his words. It was a moment of quiet revelation, a glimpse into the timeless wisdom that Mr. Kolinsky embodied.

I started to feel as though I was beginning to understand what Mr kolinsky had been trying to share with me after all this time, being exposed to all this infinite wisdom i was able to have many profound conversations with Mr kolinsky, conversations that seemed daring to bring up or scary to venture, but when i did i was greeted with a beautiful conversation, somewhat harmonious. Simmilar to that of the remarkable symphony of a classical band creating effortless, beauty within music.

As the years passed, I witnessed the inevitable passage of time in the lines on Mr. Kolinsky's face and the slight tremor in his hand. Yet, his spirit remained undiminished, a testament to the resilience of the human soul.

One day, as we walked through the garden, I asked, "Mr. Kolinsky, how do you face the inevitability of change with such grace? It's something I struggle with."

He looked out at the blooming flowers and the vibrant foliage, a smile playing at the corners of his lips. "Change, dear one, is the heartbeat of life. It reminds us that we are part of a grand symphony, each note significant in its own right. Embrace it, for within change lies the promise of new beginnings and fresh perspectives."

His words were like a soothing balm to my restless heart. I realized that in accepting change, I was not losing something but gaining the opportunity for growth and transformation.

As the years went by, I continued to cherish every moment with Mr. Kolinsky, knowing that our time together was a precious gift. It was during one of our final conversations that he looked at me with a twinkle in his eye and said, "My dear friend, the time has come for you to spread your wings and share the wisdom you've gained."

I felt a mixture of gratitude and sadness. "But how can I ever repay you for all that you've given me?"

He placed a hand on my shoulder, his touch warm and reassuring. "The greatest gift you can give is to pass on what you've learned, to be a source of guidance and inspiration for others. The journey of a seeker never truly ends; it merely transforms into something new."

And so, with a heart full of gratitude and a sense of purpose, I set forth to share the lessons I had learned from Mr. Kolinsky, knowing that his legacy would live on in every life I touched.

In the years that followed, I dedicated myself to teaching and mentoring, carrying forward the wisdom that had been bestowed upon me. I watched with joy as my students grew, their eyes alight with the same thirst for knowledge that had once burned within me.

And though Mr. Kolinsky had long since passed on, his presence felt as real to me as the air I breathed. His teachings echoed in my mind, a constant source of guidance and inspiration.

As I looked back on the journey that had brought me to this moment, I realized that life was indeed a beautiful tapestry, woven with threads of love, learning, and the enduring power of human connection.

In the years that followed, I found myself in the role of both teacher and student, for the journey of learning is a perpetual circle. I continued to seek knowledge from books, from nature, and from the experiences that life offered.

One day, a young student approached me with eager eyes and a heart hungry for understanding. "How do I begin this journey of self-discovery?" he asked.

I smiled, seeing a reflection of my own youthful curiosity in his gaze. "Begin with an open heart and a curious mind. Embrace the world around you, and never shy away from asking questions. Remember, the answers you seek are often hidden in the most unexpected places."

As I watched him embark on his own path of discovery, I was reminded of the words Mr. Kolinsky had spoken to me all those years ago. The legacy of wisdom continued, passed from one seeker to another.

As the years danced by, I witnessed the ever-changing tapestry of life with a newfound appreciation. Each season brought its own beauty, its own lessons.

In the vibrant bloom of spring, I saw the promise of new beginnings and the importance of nurturing tender shoots of growth.

The warmth of summer taught me the value of basking in the fullness of life, of embracing the joys that came my way.

Autumn's golden hues spoke of the beauty of letting go, of allowing the old to gracefully make way for the new.

And in the quiet of winter, I found solace in the restful embrace of introspection, knowing that within the stillness, the seeds of future blooms lay dormant.

Life has a way of weaving unexpected connections, of bringing kindred souls together on the journey. I met people from all walks of life, each one leaving an indelible mark on the fabric of my existence.

There was Maria, whose laughter was like a melody that echoed through the years. Her joie de vivre was a reminder that even in the face of adversity, one could choose joy.

And then there was Samuel, a quiet philosopher whose words held a depth of wisdom that belied his years. He taught me that true understanding often lies in the spaces between words.

These souls, and so many others, became threads in the tapestry of my life, adding their unique colors and textures to the ever-unfolding story.

In the twilight of my years, I often found myself returning to the garden where it all began. The memories of those early days with Mr. Kolinsky were etched in every leaf and petal.

As I sat on the familiar bench, I could almost hear his voice in the rustle of the leaves, offering gentle guidance and unwavering support.

I marveled at how the garden had evolved, much like the journey of a seeker. New blooms had replaced the old, and yet, the essence remained unchanged.

In that sacred space, I felt a profound sense of gratitude—for the lessons, for the connections, and for the enduring legacy of wisdom that would continue to ripple through time.

As the years rolled on, I felt the weight of time in my bones, a comforting weight, for it carried with it the richness of experience and the depth of understanding.

It was then that I knew it was time to pass on the torch of wisdom, to share the lessons I had learned with those who sought their own path.

I gathered a group of eager minds, much like the one I once was, and invited them to the garden. Under the dappled sunlight and the watchful gaze of ancient trees, I began to speak.

"Life is a journey of self-discovery," I told them. "It's a journey of learning, growing, and embracing the beauty that surrounds us. It's a journey that you must walk with an open heart and a curious spirit."

Their eyes sparkled with a mixture of anticipation and reverence, and I knew that the legacy would continue, that the circle of wisdom would keep turning.

As the days passed, I found myself becoming more attuned to the subtle rhythms of life. The rustling leaves in the garden seemed to whisper secrets of the universe, and the gentle hum of nature's orchestra became my daily companion.

One afternoon, Mr. Kolinsky and I sat beneath the sprawling oak tree, the dappled sunlight playing on our faces. He turned to me, his eyes sparkling with a knowing twinkle. "Ben, have you ever stopped to wonder about the infinite possibilities that tomorrow holds?"

I furrowed my brow, intrigued by his question. "What do you mean, Mr. Kolinsky?"

He leaned back, gazing up at the azure sky. "Tomorrow is a canvas waiting to be painted with the strokes of our choices. It's a blank page upon which we write the stories of our lives. And the beauty of it, Ben, is that we hold the brush, we hold the pen."

As autumn arrived, the garden transformed into a kaleidoscope of reds, oranges, and golds. The air grew crisper, carrying with it the scent of fallen leaves and the promise of change.

One evening, Mr. Kolinsky and I took a leisurely stroll through the garden, our footsteps creating a soft rhythm on the gravel path. The setting sun cast long, dramatic shadows that seemed to dance around us.

Mr. Kolinsky paused, his eyes fixed on the shifting patterns of light and dark. "Life, Ben, is much like this dance of shadows. There are moments of brightness and moments of obscurity, but both are necessary for the beauty of the whole."

I nodded, understanding dawning upon me. The highs and lows, the triumphs and tribulations—they were all part of the intricate tapestry of life. Embracing both was the key to truly experiencing its richness.

His words hung in the air, filled with a sense of both wonder and responsibility. I felt a surge of determination coursing through me. Tomorrow wasn't just another day; it was a chance to shape my destiny.

The thought stayed with me long after our conversation ended. That night, as I lay in bed, I allowed my imagination to run wild. I envisioned a future where every choice, every action, was a deliberate stroke on the canvas of my life. It was a heady feeling, the sense of agency and purpose coursing through my veins.

From that moment on, I approached each day with newfound vigour. I greeted each sunrise with anticipation, eager to add another layer to the masterpiece of my existence. And in those moments of decision, I paused, mindful of the brush in my hand and the power it held.

With each step, I let the wisdom of Mr. Kolinsky's words sink in. It was a lesson in acceptance, a reminder that every phase of life had its own unique beauty. Even in moments of darkness, there was a certain magic, a potential for growth and transformation.

In the weeks that followed, I found myself navigating life's twists and turns with a newfound grace. When challenges arose, I didn't shy away from them; instead, I embraced them as integral parts of my journey. Each shadow held the promise of illumination, and I moved forward with a sense of purpose, knowing that both light and dark were essential threads in the fabric of my story.

As autumn arrived, the garden transformed into a kaleidoscope of reds, oranges, and golds. The air grew crisper, carrying with it the scent of fallen leaves and the promise of change.

One evening, Mr. Kolinsky and I took a leisurely stroll through the garden, our footsteps creating a soft rhythm on the gravel path. The setting sun cast long, dramatic shadows that seemed to dance around us.

Mr. Kolinsky paused, his eyes fixed on the shifting patterns of light and dark. "Life, Ben, is much like this dance of shadows. There are moments of brightness and moments of obscurity, but both are necessary for the beauty of the whole."
I nodded, understanding dawning upon me. The highs and lows, the triumphs and tribulations—they were all part of the intricate tapestry of life. Embracing both was the key to truly experiencing its richness.

With each step, I let the wisdom of Mr. Kolinsky's words sink in. It was a lesson in acceptance, a reminder that every phase of life had its own unique beauty. Even in moments of darkness, there was a certain magic, a potential for growth and transformation.

In the weeks that followed, I found myself navigating life's twists and turns with a newfound grace. When challenges arose, I didn't shy away from them; instead, I embraced them as integral parts of my journey. Each shadow held the promise of illumination, and I moved forward with a sense of purpose, knowing that both light and dark were essential threads in the fabric of my story.

As winter descended, blanketing the garden in a hushed stillness, Mr. Kolinsky and I continued our daily meetings. The cold air seemed to sharpen our senses, and the world took on a crystalline clarity.

One morning, as we sat in our usual spot, I couldn't help but reflect on the wealth of wisdom Mr. Kolinsky had shared with me. His teachings weren't confined to textbooks or lectures; they were woven into the very fabric of his being.

I turned to him, gratitude swelling in my heart. "Mr. Kolinsky, you've given me more than knowledge. You've given me a compass for navigating life's intricate pathways."

He smiled, his eyes crinkling at the corners. "Ben, wisdom isn't something to be hoarded; it's meant to be shared. As you continue on your journey, remember to pass on the echoes of what you've learned."

His words resonated within me, igniting a sense of purpose. I knew that I carried not only my own dreams and aspirations but also the collective wisdom of those who had guided me.

In the days that followed, I sought opportunities to share the insights I had gained. Whether through conversations with friends or through written words, I endeavored to pass on the torch of wisdom. It was a way of honoring not only Mr. Kolinsky but all the mentors who had shaped me.

And as I watched others absorb these lessons, I realized the true power of wisdom—it had the capacity to ripple through time, leaving a lasting imprint on the souls it touched.

With the arrival of spring, the garden burst into a riot of colors, as if celebrating the renewal of life. The air was fragrant with the scent of blooming flowers, and the gentle hum of bees provided a soothing backdrop.

One day, as I wandered through the garden, I stumbled upon a secluded corner where a cluster of cherry blossoms swayed in the breeze. Their delicate petals seemed to hold the promise of new beginnings.

I thought of Mr. Kolinsky and the profound impact he had on my life. Like the blossoms, he had ushered in a season of growth and transformation, reminding me that life was an ever-evolving tapestry of moments.

As I stood there, I made a silent vow to carry forward the lessons I had learned from him. Just as spring unfurled its petals, I would embrace each new day with an open heart, ready to receive the gifts it held.

In the weeks that followed, I approached each day with a renewed sense of purpose. I allowed myself to be present in every moment, to fully experience the richness of life unfolding around me. Just like the blossoms, I too was in the midst of a blossoming—a continuous journey of growth and self-discovery.

As I sat in the garden one evening, watching the sun dip below the horizon, I couldn't help but marvel at the journey I had undertaken. The pages of my story were filled with the ink of experiences, each one a brushstroke in the painting of my life.

Mr. Kolinsky joined me, his presence a comforting anchor. "Ben, life is an exploration of the unknown. It's about stepping into uncharted territory, armed with the wisdom you've gathered along the way."

I looked at him, gratitude filling my gaze. "Thank you, Mr. Kolinsky. You've been my guiding light, illuminating the path ahead."

He placed a hand on my shoulder, his touch steady and reassuring.

"Remember, Ben, the most beautiful chapters are often written in the ink of uncertainty. Embrace the unknown, for it holds the potential for your greatest discoveries."

And with those words, I faced tomorrow with a newfound sense of purpose, ready to continue the journey, pen in hand, and heart open to the adventures that awaited.

As I immersed myself in the world of learning and growth, I found myself drawn to the concept of gratitude. It was a theme that had been subtly woven into many of Mr. Kolinsky's teachings.

One day, as we sat in the garden, sipping tea, I turned to him and asked,
"Mr. Kolinsky, what role does gratitude play in living a fulfilling life?"

He set down his cup and gazed out at the blooming flowers.

"Gratitude, my dear friend, is the foundation of a contented heart. It's the practice of recognizing and appreciating the goodness that surrounds us, even in the midst of challenges."

His words resonated with me deeply. I realized that in my pursuit of knowledge and growth, I had sometimes overlooked the simple yet profound act of being grateful for the present moment.

Mr. Kolinsky encouraged me to cultivate a daily gratitude practice. He explained that taking a few moments each day to acknowledge the blessings in our lives could lead to a greater sense of peace and fulfillment.

As the seasons changed, I found myself reflecting on the inevitability of change. It was a topic that Mr. Kolinsky had touched upon in our conversations, and one that I grappled with personally.

One crisp autumn afternoon, I asked him,

"Mr. Kolinsky, how does one navigate the complexities of change, especially when it brings uncertainty and upheaval?"

He looked at me with a knowing smile.

"Change, my dear friend, is the only constant in life. It's the river that carries us forward, whether we choose to float along or resist its current. Embracing change allows us to grow, evolve, and discover new facets of ourselves."

His words offered me a new perspective. Instead of fearing change, I began to see it as a natural and necessary part of the human experience. I learned to adapt, to flow with the currents of life, and to find beauty in the ever-shifting landscape.

As I delved deeper into my journey of self-discovery, I encountered the profound wisdom of letting go. It was a concept that had eluded me for much of my life, but one that I knew was essential for my growth.

One evening, under the canvas of a twilight sky, I mustered the courage to ask Mr. Kolinsky,

"How does one master the art of letting go? How do you release attachments to the past or expectations for the future?"

He regarded me with gentle eyes.
"Letting go, my dear friend, is an act of surrendering the need for control. It's about releasing the grip on what was or what could be, and fully embracing what is. It's a profound trust in the flow of life."

His words held a transformative power.
I began to practice letting go in small moments, allowing life to unfold without my attempts to dictate its course. I discovered a newfound freedom in surrendering to the rhythm of existence.

As the days turned into months, I marveled at the intricate web of connections that wove through our lives. It was a theme that had become increasingly evident in my conversations with Mr. Kolinsky.

One afternoon, as we sat in the garden, I asked him, "Mr. Kolinsky, what is the true significance of the connections we form with others? How do they shape our journey?"

He looked at me with a twinkle in his eye.

"Connections, my dear friend, are the threads that bind us to the tapestry of humanity. They are the notes in the symphony of life, each one contributing to the beauty of the whole. Through our connections, we learn, grow, and find reflections of ourselves in others."

His words resonated deeply within me. I began to cherish the connections I had forged on this journey, recognizing that they were not mere chance encounters, but purposeful meetings that enriched my path.

In the midst of my journey, I found myself confronting the concept of vulnerability. It was a theme that had quietly woven itself through the tapestry of my experiences, waiting to be acknowledged.

One evening, as the garden was bathed in the soft glow of twilight, I turned to Mr. Kolinsky.

"Mr. Kolinsky, how does one find the courage to be vulnerable, to open their heart even when it feels risky?"

He regarded me with a solemn yet kind expression.

"Vulnerability, my dear friend, is the gateway to authentic connection. It's the act of baring your soul, of allowing others to witness your true self. In that space of vulnerability, we find the deepest forms of understanding and empathy."

His words struck a chord within me. I realized that my journey of self-discovery was intricately tied to my willingness to be vulnerable, to embrace both my strengths and my imperfections.

As my understanding of life's intricacies deepened, I returned to the question of purpose. It was a topic that had been a steady undercurrent in my conversations with Mr. Kolinsky.

One cool spring afternoon, I asked him, "Mr. Kolinsky, how does one reconcile the ebb and flow of purpose? How do we navigate moments of clarity and moments of uncertainty?"

He turned to me with a knowing smile.

"Purpose, my dear friend, is not a fixed destination, but a fluid journey. It's not a singular calling, but a series of callings that evolve with time. Embrace the moments of clarity, and trust that the moments of uncertainty are simply opportunities for growth."

His words offered me a newfound perspective on the ever-changing nature of purpose. I began to see it not as a distant beacon, but as a guiding star that illuminated my path step by step.

As the years unfolded, I found myself immersed in the symphony of dreams. It was a theme that had quietly woven itself into the fabric of my existence, urging me to listen.

One starlit summer night, I asked Mr. Kolinsky, "Mr. Kolinsky, what is the significance of our dreams? How do they shape our journey?"

He gazed up at the night sky, where the stars seemed to wink knowingly.
"Dreams, my dear friend, are the whispers of our deepest desires. They are the seeds of potential waiting to be nurtured. Pay attention to your dreams, for they hold the keys to unlocking your fullest potential."

His words stirred something within me. I began to honor my dreams not as mere flights of fancy, but as sacred messages from the depths of my soul.

As I stood on the threshold of a new chapter, I looked back on the rich tapestry of my journey. Each chapter, each moment, had contributed to the intricate design of my existence.

I knew that there were still uncharted territories ahead, adventures that awaited my discovery. With Mr. Kolinsky's wisdom as my compass, I felt an unshakeable sense of readiness.

As the sun painted the sky in hues of gold and rose, I closed my eyes and took a moment to breathe. I felt the pulse of life around me, the ever-present rhythm that connected us all.

With a heart full of gratitude, I stepped forward, eager to embrace the next chapters of the ever-unfolding tapestry of life.

As the days turned into months and the seasons changed, my journey of self-discovery and growth continued. I learned valuable lessons about compassion, forgiveness, purpose, and the relentless pursuit of knowledge.

I also discovered that the true essence of life lay in the connections we formed with others, in the wisdom we gained from those who walked before us, and in the love and understanding we shared with fellow travellers on this journey.

My bond with Mr. Kolinsky grew stronger with each passing day, and I knew that I had found not only a teacher but a mentor, a friend, and a guiding light on my path.

And so, our story continued, filled with conversations under the open sky, moments of revelation, and the enduring belief that life was a beautiful journey meant to be embraced, explored, and cherished.

As I looked ahead to the horizon, I knew that the road of self-discovery stretched far beyond what I could see. But with Mr. Kolinsky by my side, I felt ready to face whatever challenges and adventures lay ahead.

He looked at me with a twinkle in his eye.

"Connections, my dear friend, are the threads that bind us to the tapestry of humanity. They are the notes in the symphony of life, each one contributing to the beauty of the whole. Through our connections, we learn, grow, and find reflections of ourselves in others."

His words resonated deeply within me. I began to cherish the connections I had forged on this journey, recognizing that they were not mere chance encounters, but purposeful meetings that enriched my path.

In the quiet moments of reflection, I often found myself revisiting the wisdom Mr. Kolinsky had shared. His words resonated within me, becoming the guiding stars of my journey. Each piece of advice was like a beacon, illuminating the path I walked.

As we sat in the garden one afternoon, a gentle breeze rustling the leaves, I turned to Mr. Kolinsky.
"Your wisdom, it's like an echo in my soul. Your teachings have become a part of me."

He smiled, his eyes crinkling at the corners.

"Ben, true wisdom isn't found in the words themselves, but in how they find a home within you. It's in the way they shape your thoughts, your actions, and the person you're becoming."

And in that moment, I understood that wisdom wasn't merely a collection of knowledge, but a living force that could transform a life.

In the garden's quiet embrace, I learned the art of patience. Each bloom unfurled in its own time, and every season had its purpose. It was a dance of nature, a rhythm of waiting and growth.

One day, as I marveled at a bud on the verge of blossoming, Mr. Kolinsky spoke,

"Patience, Ben, is not about idly waiting, but about trusting the process. It's about understanding that growth takes time, and that every moment, even the ones spent in anticipation, holds its own beauty."

And so, I learned to dance with patience, to trust in the unfolding of my own journey.

Life, I realized, was a vast tapestry woven from the threads of experience. Every joy, every sorrow, every triumph, and every stumble contributed to the masterpiece.

As I shared this revelation with Mr. Kolinsky, he nodded in agreement.
"Our experiences, Ben, are the colors that give depth and meaning to the fabric of our lives. Embrace each thread, for it has a part to play in the beauty of the whole."

And from then on, I learned to honor not only the grand moments, but also the subtle threads that wove the intricate pattern of my existence.

The future, I realized, was a vast expanse of the unknown. It stretched beyond the horizon, waiting to be explored. It was both thrilling and daunting, for it held the promise of new discoveries and the challenge of uncharted territory.

One evening, as the sun dipped below the horizon, casting the sky in hues of gold and pink, I turned to Mr. Kolinsky.

"The unknown, Mr. Kolinsky, it's both exhilarating and a little frightening. How do you navigate it?"

He gazed at the horizon, his eyes filled with a quiet knowing. "Embrace it, Ben. The unknown is where adventure resides. It's where you'll find the unexpected gifts that life has in store for you. Trust in the journey, and have faith that each step will lead you exactly where you need to be."

And so, I stepped forward into the unknown, my heart brimming with anticipation.

In the garden's sanctuary, I discovered the profound joy of giving. Whether it was tending to the blooms, lending a listening ear, or simply offering a kind word, I found that giving was a melody that resonated deep within my soul.

One morning, as we worked side by side in the garden, I said to Mr. Kolinsky, "The act of giving, it feels like a symphony, a harmonious exchange of energy and goodwill."

He smiled, his hands cradling a delicate bloom. "Giving, Ben, is a gift in itself. It connects us to the essence of humanity, reminding us that we are all bound together in this beautiful tapestry of life."

And from that moment on, I vowed to let the symphony of giving be the song that guided my days.

In the garden's sanctuary, I discovered the profound joy of giving. Whether it was tending to the blooms, lending a listening ear, or simply offering a kind word, I found that giving was a melody that resonated deep within my soul.
One morning, as we worked side by side in the garden, I said to Mr. Kolinsky,

"The act of giving, it feels like a symphony, a harmonious exchange of energy and goodwill."
He smiled, his hands cradling a delicate bloom.
"Giving, Ben, is a gift in itself. It connects us to the essence of humanity, reminding us that we are all bound together in this beautiful tapestry of life."

And from that moment on, I vowed to let the symphony of giving be the song that guided my days.

As the seasons turned, I witnessed the garden's transformation. Each bloom, though fleeting, left a legacy of beauty. It was a poignant reminder that even the briefest moments could leave an indelible mark.

One day, as I stood amidst the blooms, I turned to Mr. Kolinsky. "The garden, it teaches us about legacy, doesn't it? About the impact we leave behind, no matter how small."

He nodded, his eyes reflecting the wisdom of years. "Indeed, Ben. A life well lived, no matter how humble, leaves a legacy of love, wisdom, and beauty. It's a gift to the world and a testament to the richness of the human spirit."

And in that moment, I knew that the legacy I wished to leave was one of kindness, of learning, and of a heart open to the beauty of the world.

In the tranquil moments of the garden, I often found myself listening to the whispers of the wind. It carried with it secrets of the world, stories of distant lands, and the promise of endless adventures.

One evening, as the garden basked in the golden hues of sunset, I turned to Mr. Kolinsky.
"The wind, Mr. Kolinsky, it's like a messenger from places unseen. It reminds me of the vastness of the world."

He gazed into the horizon, his eyes dancing with the play of shadows. "The world, Ben, is a tapestry of stories waiting to be told. The wind carries those tales, and if you listen closely, you'll find that you're a part of them too."

And from then on, I paid heed to the whispers of the wind, knowing that they carried the echoes of a world waiting to be explored.

Among the blooms, I discovered a language that transcended words. Each petal held a message, a story of growth, of beauty, and of the fleeting nature of moments.

One afternoon, as we meandered through the garden, I said to Mr. Kolinsky,

"The blooms, they speak a language all their own. It's as if they're whispering secrets of life."

He nodded, his fingers grazing the velvety petals of a rose. "The language of blooms, Ben, is a silent poetry. It reminds us to cherish each moment, for like the petals, they are here for a brief, beautiful moment, and then they are gone."

And from then on, I listened to the language of blooms, finding solace in their silent wisdom.

In the garden's rhythm, I witnessed the dance of resilience. Each bloom, though delicate, stood tall in the face of wind and rain. It was a testament to nature's unyielding spirit.

As I marveled at a particularly steadfast bloom, I turned to Mr. Kolinsky.

"Resilience, Mr. Kolinsky, it's a quality that seems woven into the very fabric of this garden."

He smiled, his eyes twinkling with a quiet pride. "Nature, Ben, is a master teacher of resilience. It reminds us that even in the midst of challenges, there is a strength within us waiting to bloom."

And from then on, I carried with me the dance of resilience, knowing that it was a quality that could carry me through the storms of life.

As the days turned into months, I marveled at the intricate web of connections that wove through our lives. It was a theme that had become increasingly evident in my conversations with Mr. Kolinsky.

One afternoon, as we sat in the garden, I asked him,
"Mr. Kolinsky, what is the true significance of the connections we form with others? How do they shape our journey?"

He looked at me with a twinkle in his eye.
"Connections, my dear friend, are the threads that bind us to the tapestry of humanity. They are the notes in the symphony of life, each one contributing to the beauty of the whole. Through our connections, we learn, grow, and find reflections of ourselves in others."

His words resonated deeply within me. I began to cherish the connections I had forged on this journey, recognizing that they were not mere chance encounters, but purposeful meetings that enriched my path.

As the seasons wove their tapestry, I marveled at the ever-changing landscape of the garden. Each bloom, each leaf, played its part in the grand design.

One morning, as I stood amidst the colors and fragrances, I turned to Mr. Kolinsky. "The garden, Mr. Kolinsky, it's a living testament to the beauty of change. It reminds me that life is an ever-unfolding tapestry."

He nodded, his gaze sweeping over the blooms. "Indeed, Ben. Change is woven into the very fabric of existence. Embrace it, for it is the loom on which the tapestry of life is woven."

And from then on, I welcomed change as a dear friend, knowing that it was the artist's brushstroke on the canvas of life.

With each passing day, the garden became not only a place of solace but a canvas of inspiration. Every bloom, every rustling leaf, held a lesson, a story, a reminder that life's journey was meant to be embraced.

As I sat beside Mr. Kolinsky one evening, the sky ablaze with the hues of sunset, I said to him, "The journey, Mr. Kolinsky, it feels like an endless adventure, with something new to discover at every turn."

He turned to me, his eyes kindling with a familiar spark. "Ben, my dear friend, the journey is the destination. It's in the seeking, the learning, the growing, that we truly live."

And so, our journey continued, a tapestry of moments woven with threads of wisdom, laughter, and the quiet beauty of the garden.

About The Author

AS HEARD ON RADIO & AS SEEN ON TV & IN
NEWSPAPERS & MAGAZINES

Purpose: To inspire 1 million young people
to explore their internal and external world
through the teaching of self-discovery,
exploration and engineering planting one
seed at a time

Paolo was a moderator for 10x Kids which is
hosted by Sabrina & Scarlett Cardone.

Websites:
https://linktr.ee/AuthorPaolobensalmi

2021 Paolo was a guest speaker on for the UN
(United Nations) Global Goals 2030 thanks to
I AM The Code founder Lady Marieme Jamme

Podcast Show Host of Life according To
Paolo:
https://paolobensalmi.sounder.fm/show/life-
according-to-paolo

Paolo is the youngest ever Water-to-Go
Ambassador:
WWW.WATERTOGO.EU/PARTNERSHIPS/PAOL
OBENSALMI

Paolo was chosen to develop UnLtd application process together with his mother, big brother and big sister

Paolo Ben Salmi is a 13-year-old personal development coach and founder of Pint Size Adventurer. Paolo is here to help you plant the seed toward self-discovery, exploration of the internal and external world. Paolo offers a variety of products and services to assist you to create a brighter future. His desire is to encourage as many children as possible to go on adventures both internally and externally to activate their natural curiosity.

Paolo Ben Salmi aka The Tree Whisper Fruit Forest steward in Tanzania (he planted 10,000 trees) ■: Borg Global Holdings – Forest Nation Forests. Paolo Ben Salmi aka The Tree Whisper fruit forest steward in Tanzania ■: <u>Borg Global Holdings – ForestNation Forests</u>

Brunel University London (B.U.L) has given the Ben Salmi family the opportunity to participate in Masterclasses covering Engineering, Computer Science and currently the Environmental Agency Masterclass.

Paolos youngest brother 7 year old Amire is proud to be the youngest ever honorary STEM Ambassador in history for Brunel University London (B.U.L).

B.U.L has given the homeschooled families the opportunity to participate in masterclasses for the first time in history thanks to Lesley Warren.

Paolo has interviewed people like Ari Rastegar, Harry Hugo, Travis W Fox, Douglas Vermeeren, Bernardodo Mayo, Bob Doyle, Meagen Fettes, Udo Erasmus and Dr John Demartini to name a few.

Paolo Ben Salmi is an award-winning publisher and author of the book series called 'Pint Size Adventurer - 10 Keys Principles to Get Your Kids off their iPads & Into the Wild.'
Paolo is an Award-Winning public speaker, publisher, author and visionary, who has spoken at venues such as Mercedes Benz World, Chelsea FC and Virgin Money alongside his family.

My family and I have been acknowledged in the credits of a NEW movie called: How Thoughts Become Things movie promotional link:

Bit.ly/HowThoughtsBecomeThingsMovie2020

Water-to-Go blog about Paolo:
https://www.watertogo.eu/blog/meet-paolo-water-to-gos-youngest-ever-ambassador/

Paolo is the founder of his own publishing house called Adventurous Publishing.

Paolo hosted his signature program called Pint Size Adventurer - The Abundant Adventure Creator™ at the prestigious Virgin Money Lounge:
London Haymarket: Pint Size Adventurer - The Abundant Adventure Creator - My Virgin Money

Paolo Ben Salmi is an award-winning author of the book series called Pint Size Adventurer - 10 Keys Principles to Get Your KIDS off their iPads & Into the Wild.

BEN SALMI FAMILY MANTRA

"BEN SALMI TEAMWORK MAKES THE DREAMWORK

We believe that there is no such thing as failure only feedback.

We also believe that the journey of one thousand miles begins with a single step in the right direction

FAMILY ANTHEM

If you want to be somebody,
If you want to go somewhere,
You better wake up and PAY ATTENTION

I'm ready to be somebody,
I'm ready to go somewhere,
I'm ready to wake up and PAY ATTENTION!

The question is ARE YOU?